Poetry - a tasting

Sarah Webster

Presentation by *BookLeaf Publishing*

Web: www.bookleafpub.com

E-mail: info@bookleafpub.com

ISBN: 9789357616713

First edition 2022

To Tony P, for encouraging and inspiring me to write. I hope my writing is as impactful as yours; maybe one day!

PREFACE

After a moment's split decision, I signed up for a 21-day poetry writing challenge. Having never written poetry before, it was certainly a steep learning curve! I hope you enjoy the result as much as I enjoyed the process.

Spring

Warm breeze caresses,
Fragrant blossoms in the air
Spring, finally here

Sunshine

Sunshine: warm, playful
Golden rays across my skin
Basking in its warmth

Changing Seasons

Winter
Gloomy, grey
Sleeping, hiding, waiting
Coats, fire, hats, water
Riding, swimming, gardening
Bright, balmy
Summer

Night Sky

Fiery orange
Fading to a mystic pink
Purple, blue, then night

Sunrise

5

Orange through the clouds
Buildings are silhouetted
Sky blue all around

The Storm

Thunder rumbles across the landscape,
Setting an ominous tone.

The heavy gloomy sky,
Looms low, threatening with rain.

Grey clouds tumbling and crashing,
Racing to escape one another.

Lightning flashes far and near,
Illuminating the dull, dark scene.

Wind howls ferociously
A wild beast straining to be released.

The storm is coming; the storm is here.

Water: A love-hate relationship

Water; the elixir of life.
Without it we could perish.
Yet, it cruelly taunts us.

Staying just out of reach,
As it dehydrates the land, the people, the
animals, the plants.
Thirsts go unquenched; crops brown, shrivel and
expire.

Or, it smothers us in its grasp.
"You want me?" it seems to say, "You really
want me?"
Be careful what you wish for. Too much of a
good thing.

Cascading over hills and through valleys.
Sometimes rising slowly, but often in raging
torrents.
Forever changing landscapes, destroying
livelihoods, wiping out towns.

The Garden

Garden
Green, peaceful
Growing, reaching, climbing
Birds, bees, insects, bugs
Sprouting, flowering, thriving
Rewarding, nourishing
Sanctuary

Blood, sweat, tears: garden

Back and forth and back we go
Hauling the loads to and fro.
Dirt, dirt dirt; more dirt!
Sweat patches gather on our shirt

Put it there, no put it here,
Plants are swapped round far and near.
Too much space? Not enough!
Too much sun? Wind's too rough!

If conditions aren't quite right
Not a veg will be in sight; despite
Reading information cards,
Thinking, pond'ring long and hard.

Hours pass, the sun gets hot,
Finally the plants are in their spots,
Watering, feeding, mulching, training,
Similar to child-raising!

Slowly, surely buds appear
New growth happens, shed a tear!
Tracking, checking, is that new?
The marigolds are growing too!

Lettuce, beans, and snow peas too,
There's even a tiny carrot or two!
A bounty to share as friends partake,
How'd we do it? T'was a piece of cake!

Release the Plants!

Slowly, tenderly, released from their
confinement
Unfolding and stretching, enjoying their
freedoms.
Shaken loose and delicately separated,
A brief moment before they are settled in their
new, spacious homes, not too far from their
neighbours.

Noises of the Neighbourhood

Wee-wor, Wee-wor, WEE-WOR, WEE-WOR,
wee-wor, wee-wor…
Ding, ding…. Ding, ding, ding.. DING DING,
DING DING DING DING DING!!!
BWWARP! Bang, bang, bang, whirr, whirr
Honk! HOOOOONNNNKK! Beep beep!
VROOMMMM!!!

Tweet, tweet, coo, coo, squawk squawk!
Buzz, buzz, buzz, buzz
Woof, woof, howl, howl
Scratch, scratch, meow, meow

Wah! Wah! Giggle, giggle
Oi! Watch where you're going!
Hello! Oh my gosh, so nice to see you!
I think there's a café down here…

My Neighbourhood

Cute cats seeking pats
Green and leafy avenues
Kids riding their bikes.

Coffee and cafes
Every kind of restaurant
A foodie's haven

Community groups
Looking after another
Keeping it local.

An Ode to Cake

Cake: such a simple little word
Brings such joy once it is heard.
Kuchen, gateau, queque, taart
Every language plays a part.

Cake comes in every shape and size,
Such a choice; a feast for the eyes.
Round, loaf, cupcakes, square
Multi-tiered if you so dare.

Breakfast, morning tea and lunch
Definitely part of brunch.
An afternoon pick me up,
Can be made even in a cup.

Moist texture, dense and sweet
Such decadence! What a treat!
Cream and frosting oozing out,
Pleasure eating is what cake's all about.

And so this ode to cake is here,
For all cake-lovers, far and near.
Just imagine what life would be like,
If we didn't have cake; I'd go on strike!

Coffee

Oh coffee, saviour of mornings!
The tantalising aroma,
Wafting through the air,
Will drag even the grumpiest
From his lair.

Oh coffee, saviour of mornings!
The fragrant steam drifting lazily upward,
Enveloped by your favourite mug.
Warm, familiar, and comforting,
It really is just like a hug.

Oh coffee, savour of mornings!
Black, latte, cold drip, espresso
Mocha, flat white, affogato.
Cappuccino, Americano,
Oh coffee, saviour of mornings!

Exploring

Back roads are beckoning,
Gravel, dust, trees, sky.
Away from the hustle; deep breaths
Senses awakening.

Hiking boots laced up,
No track too muddy.
Climbing to the top,
A different perspective.

Trying new foods,
Attempting the language.
Different cultures,
Ready for something different.

Cities and towns,
Nature and animals,
Crazy adventures,
Taking it slow.

Travel

Travel
Exciting, new
Walking, flying, sailing
Food, sights, people, culture
Eating, drinking, laughing, dancing
Eye-opening, life-changing
Travel

Escape to Another World

Rough streets of London
Or sunny California,
The English countryside,
Sydney Australia.

Escaping an assassin
Or solving a murder,
Finding yourself in therapy,
Downing cocktails on the beach.

So many places to explore,
So many adventures to be had.
Reading brings endless journeys
Adding richness and knowledge for life.

Lonely, but not alone

19

Crowds of hundreds push past on the street,
Lonely, but not alone.

312 Facebook friends awaiting,
Lonely, but not alone.

Team morning teas, lunches and coffee runs
Lonely, but not alone.

A complex of 150 residents surrounds,
Lonely, but not alone.

Flies

Buzzing through the air,
That familiar summertime sound.
Circling and loitering,
They are always heard around.

Landing on the pav,
The salad and the steak.
A quick lap round the table,
And now they're on the cake!

We see them just as pesky pests,
But they are unsung heroes.
They pollinate and eat our waste,
Devouring it by kilos.

So next time have a stop and think
When you're about to swat.
Although annoying in our lives
They really mean a lot!

"Dad Jokes"

Can cause a loud groan
But usually a giggle
Can't live without them

The End!

That was a learning curve
Helps to have a thesaurus
Enjoyed it nonetheless

Even though it was tough to finds time
Not sure I'd do it again
Done and dusted!